For David Carter Dickson

Contents

Origin of the Species

Infrareal

Laureate

Larry's Requiem for Uncle Burton

Acknowledgments

Origin of the Species

Larry's Anecdotal Evidence 97

So they just kept having kids
and they all looked just like them,
same fearful eyes, flat foreheads,
jug-eared as mules.
They all wore overalls
and whatever shoes
they got from the church
that came to their holler
twice a year, before
the snow time
and after the spring.
When they got old enough,
they run off to find
anything or anybody else—
so came Burton and Daddy
together to here
after the war.

Time Traveler

Larry lived a week in one day,
cars flashing by, the neighbor
mowing both trailer yards in
ten minutes flat; yet Larry
rocked in regular time as
Uncle Burton's beat-to-hell
rocker argued its rhythm
on the broken slatted porch.
Larry sipped the bourbon flask
till he slept, his head tilted back,
beard up like a wiry bush.
When he awoke all stiff-necked,
the world had slowed to its
regular crawl and he shrugged
the whole day off as a dream.

Crazy Train

When we were kids, Sam was crazy for trains,
would holler till Uncle Burton pulled off
the road, and Sam would watch every last car
till the caboose creeped by and the bleached air
would slowly recover from the relentless roar,
the shook gravel around the track resettled.
It was like the power of the train released
some kind of tension in my brother,
same way I felt watching a waterfall
endlessly tumble over boulders; it
was a pleasure I had no words for and
still don't, and there are some I still hike
to and sit by and wonder how the rocks
look the same after all the gushing water
of the years. Now Sam ain't watched a freight train
in the years since he started chasing the Lord,
and I sometimes wonder just what he's lost.

Larry's Anecdotal Evidence

I could hear a train
out across the field
beyond the river gorge
in the little town.
I'd lay there in my bed,
the farm house so dark
I couldn't see nothing
but the orange eye of
the iron woodstove
in the front room.
The train whistle would
blow and I could hear
pine resin sizzle, a knot
pop as the flames licked
the sweet green wood.
Under three of Mamaw's quilts,
I'd think about hunting rabbits
Saturday morning or climbing
the bluff to the mountain,
and I'd fall asleep and dream
about wildcats and devils
and the blazing fiery pits of hell.

Larry's Anecdotal Evidence 4

Rat and Boy lived in the cement-block shack
out at the end of all the fields with their
Uncle Reep who worked for Burton and stayed drunk
most nights and weekends. When Reep died, the law came
and took Rat and Boy to the orphanage
where they gave them regular names and whipped them
for pissing their pants and smelling like animals.
Rat, as it turned out, was blind in one eye
and Boy was unable to talk, but a
newly ordained Baptist preacher and his
young wife adopted them both and moved them
into the parsonage where the preacher beat them
mercilessly for pissing their pants and smelling
like animals. The wife, nevertheless, gussied them
up and sat them on the bench behind the organ
she played each Sunday morning. The church ladies
pinched their cheeks and told them what lucky
little orphans they were. They became good little
Christians, attended the church and went to school,
though Boy could never learn a thing, and
apparently neither one ever quite got the Lord.
When he turned sixteen, Rat waited till his
parents had gone to bed and carved them up
with the butcher knife he'd been sharpening
for a week. When I shared a cell with him
at the high-rise, Rat had lost track of his brother,
and he told me that night with the butcher knife
was the best one of his life, and he wished he could
do it again.

Larry's Anecdotal Evidence 44

Christmas was never much
except when I was twelve
and Burton gave me the
rifle he bought from pawn
that I carried straight to
the woods along the bluff
and sighted every bird
and squirrel that moved but
could not pull the trigger.
I stood there an hour,
watching my breath rise up,
stock against my shoulder,
sighting down the barrel.
Years I had dreamed of this,
the thrill of my own gun.
I never told no one.

Larry's Deduction

He knew that if he worked hard
and did the right things, it would
make no difference; he had
studied Daddy and Burton
battling the sun in the fields,
wiping whole afternoons of
sweat on faded red hankies
they stuffed in back overall
pockets, the hay rake or the
tractor always broken just
before the rain, despite church
donations and prayers over
supper. Momma washed his mouth
out, but he still swore enough
for them all because he knew
there had to be some better
way than doing the right thing.

Larry's First Apocalypse

A super-red sunset swept across the sky,
a fire come down to us, Larry thought,
and he wondered where his brother was,
out at the brush piles, messing with
the copperheads, or maybe mindlessly
damming the creek for the hundredth time.
The red sky was like a lake of blood,
and it had stopped over the field
and the valley below; time stopped,
Larry was sure, and somewhere Sam
was righting an overturned wash tub
to see the black widow beneath
because he thought it beautiful,
noticing not the sky or that the
end was nigh.

Only Monsters

This is the truth.
I'm a fucking monster,
and I need to be killed
before I get worse.
The least thing sets me off.
Hate is the wrong word
to describe this emotion,
and I fear the next hour,
sometimes the next minute.
Once there was a day,
a stunningly warm day,
when teachers and professors
said, "He might be the one,"
but in their hearts they knew
better, that the warmth of
the day had fooled them,
that only monsters came
from that mill town,
from that played-out
playground.

Larry's Cosmic Epiphany

During that stretch at the high-rise,
I started to read, first the Bible,
thinking there was something there,
then books about the universe;
and I was startled to discover
just how insignificant we are,
barely a speck in the great swirl
of light and darkness,
and when I thought about
all those other planets where
life was possible, I didn't feel
the same loneliness I'd always felt
and I knew I could find a path out
of the place I'd put myself.
Nights I'd read the poems
that our teacher had left me,
and I'd think about the heavens
and how they went on and on,
far beyond the barred windows
of my little dreams.

Hay Day

The July sun bearing down on us,
hell, everybody knows what it feels like
to load the hay wagon
till your hands get bloody
from the twine cuts
and the dry stickers
while the tractor inches
one side to the other,
down and finally up,
till you lie flat on your back
atop the load and raise
the electric wire with a stick
crossing toward the barn,
and then the pure cold taste
from the dipper
in the well bucket
lifted from the stone gut
of Burton's red earth.

Larry's Anecdotal Evidence 12

So Burton got us in a church one time,
and the first thing you know, we're shepherds
in the annual Christmas program; now
Sam hated the sack robes and the head rags,
but they let us take the shepherd staffs home,
and we poked the hogs and the cows with them,
then had a violent fight by the fire pit
where Sam lost a tooth when I bucked him with
the straight end; then Daddy came home lit up
and chased me around the barn, hollering
"You're gonna pay for that tooth!"; we never
went back to do the program, but Sam would
put the robe on sometimes, pretending the
Lord was in the feed trough, and he would stand
there with the staff, saying his Bible verse,
and I shoulda known then he would one day
preach and that I couldn't knock it outta him.

Larry's Poems of Place 2

The first light beyond Burton's field
is a pink-orange sliver, a
knife-edge before the horizon's
broken egg slicks over gray sky
and day becomes like it always
was, cows called by the clocks of their
white bellies to the feed trough, and I
am a boy who breaks two bales
slicing twine with a Barlow, then
pouring a cup of sweet feed for
each blunt hard face I can still name:
Freebie, Gomer, Betsy, Otis;
grain stuck in pink nostrils, winter
steam rising as they snort, shuffle;
school waiting elsewhere to kill me.

Larry Anecdotal Evidence 73

I was thirteen or fourteen,
home by myself when the neighbor's
house caught fire, and I knew that
they were all gone to the fair.
At first I saw smoke circling
from the back side where the kitchen
bumped against the old back porch;
eventually, I saw
flames leap the peak and lap slowly
down the front side where they stacked
the firewood and the hounds liked
to lazy up in the dirt.
Then I ran outside and watched
the whole thing bloom and crackle.
When they finally got there
with the fire trucks, they was too late
and I pretended I had
been down at the creek bottom;
but they all looked at me like
they thought that I done it,
and maybe I did.

Larry's Pragma 14

"Everything happens for a reason,"
they used to tell me at the school and
on those few times I got drug to the church.
Was what the preacher said
after Burton turned the tractor over,
pulling a load of pulp across a hill,
and it was bullshit then
and it's bullshit now—
from the time this merry-go-round started:
you get on; you get off
and it will run without you
and over you and right through
your memories and ambitions,
and what we call destiny,
loading it up with meaning,
is nothing but coincidence.
So, we fought because we are here,
not because we "are here."

Larry's Anecdotal Evidence 79

My year of high school
I sat the brick wall outside the lunchroom
where the hippies and incorrigibles
aligned themselves, clenching cigarettes,
talking about concerts and cars.
At first there were some guys
that wanted to try me,
who'd heard I'd been to Jackson.
But soon they found out
how deep my heat would go,
and they knew I didn't give a damn
about their 396s or their Deep Purple
Smoke on the Water; that I was
just sitting that ugly chipped brick
at their cow shit school,
waiting patiently as I could
to turn sixteen, and they best
not get between me and my time.

Larry's Anecdotal Evidence 80

Burton told me about the death horse
when I was twelve because he'd had a vision
and knew it would come for me;
and that fall afternoon, when Uncle lay pinned
by a tractor on a hill too steep
for anything but scrubby pine,
I sat in a rocker on my trailer porch asleep,
awakened by its ghastly nickering, gray-faced
with eyes as black-red as dried blood;
and when I shuddered, it dissolved
like the pink light that shades a dream,
and I heard the sigh of Sam's pickup
and saw his head sink forward
under the weight of what
I already knew.

Larry's Anecdotal Evidence 90

I was walkin' the tower trail
on the mountain the day
I found the hanged man.
I'd go there a afternoon
some days when I was
shining on the fieldwork.
The limb that held the rope
was bent about to break.
He'd been hanging a week
and the birds had stripped
his face nearly to skull,
his bloated body in a torn
work coat. I didn't have no
cell phone then, nobody did,
so I hoofed it to Charlie's
Sunoco and told the cop lady
that answered, and you want
to know something crazy?
She actually ask me
why I thought he did it,
and I said "Why the hell does
anybody kill hisself?"
and she paused long enough
to make me wish I'd just
left that poor bastard
hanging up there for the buzzards.

Larry's Anecdotal Evidence 92

"Of course the angel is blonde,"
Sam said. "And beautiful, too?"
"Like an angel." My chair squeaked
as I leaned forward to lap
sausage gravy from my plate.
"I believe in the devil,"
I said. "She has bright blue eyes,
and she watches me asleep,
and she helps me on school tests,"
Sam said; and there was a buzz,
a whirring of wings, a sound
softer than a apostrophe,
and I wiped the gravy off
my face and reached out my hand
to touch the wings, so white they
made me wince.

Infrareal

Barn Burning

When Larry entered the fitness center,
no one asked him to swipe his card;
no one stopped him as he walked past
the rows of stationary bikes and elliptical
runners, the three-deep line of treadmills;
and when he glanced side to side at
sweaty thirtysomethings stretching lean
arms and hamstrings on the latest machines
that isolated the muscle groups perfectly,
their eyes averted; he was so clearly
a paranoid boyfriend come to kill, or
the fulfillment of revenge from
a gone-bad drug deal; his arms bulged
from the cutoff camouflage, and his boots
scuffed mud and cow shit on the scrubbed tile.
There were some bad dudes working out,
fortyish, clinging to the leavings of glory days,
but they pretended to involve themselves
with adjusting weight levels or drying their
faces with hand towels, and Larry looked at
each of them the way he would estimate
a beef calf or a shoat. When he left,
having been in some way satisfied,
the staff members sighed deeply and
the piped music seemed to return
and the rollers and pulleys and little motors
hummed again the song of the happy electric herd.

Los Larry's Pragma

The paper says there are nine billion
dollars worth of crops left in the field
this year because of new immigration laws,
and Larry remembers how they never left
anything in the field, living through
September on late tomatoes waiting
for the first cool hog-killing weather,
everything that looked like a potato
cleaned and left lying on newspaper
in Uncle Burton's basement,
even the last okra, rough and overgrown,
sliced into Mawmaw's memory soup.
Nine billion dollars hanging on trees
and vines, hidden under musty dirt.
He clicked the remote and changed
the TV to a Mexican soap opera,
but the channel was gone.

Larry's Meme

I was staying at a rent-by-the-week
in the 321 death curve outside
Boone. There was a girl I met in town
at a bar on King Street—she was with a
singer from a Jimmy Bucket cover
band—I knew he was a pussy—but, man,
he didn't even fight it—some people,
you know, are just put together easy.
Well, we're at the no-tell in the jack curve,
the only folks there not hooked on crystal,
when a big black Buick pulls in the lot,
the window rolls down slow, and this guy says
from the blackness inside the black car, "I'm
a trying to find a stolen guitar,"
and while I give him my froze-hearted look,
I'm thinking I know that voice even
as I say, "You at the wrong fucking place,"
and the window slides back shut and the car
carrying old Doc Watson clips the curb,
careening back into tourist traffic.

Larry's Mercy

"Don't take me alive," he said, hollow words
I'd heard before; even a junkie wants
to live, given the other choice, so
I stepped toward him behind the pistol,
watching him squint in the cool flashlight blast.
"What you doing out here on my land, punk?
Looking for my crop, I bet," and his face
registered then as a kid who'd bought some
pot last weekend. How could I forget? He
had Tourette's or something, made little sounds
like a dove while we sampled the hooch; so
I felt a little sorry for the kid,
generous, you might even say. "Hold your
hands out," I said, and when he did, I brought
the barrel of the pistol down across
his knuckles and he whimpered like a pup,
holding his fingers to his mouth, grunting
softly then uncontrollably, as he
staggered then ran through the trees then under
moonlight, across an abandoned corn field,
out into endless night.

Larry's Reaping

He played bull fiddle in a porch band,
Sunday afternoons, full of chicken,
fried taters, and purple lima beans.
I watched them from a church parking lot,
Sunday shirts unbuttoned to wife beaters,
silently passing a jug of white,
the mandolin tuning as one wife
poked her head through the trailer door to
shout, "I's missing a cake fork," slapping
the door back shut, catching her apron.
When I creeped the black 250 down
their drive, he looked up like a diver
who just seen a shark swim above him.
I smiled like I always do, chewing
on a piece of straw, and he left the
fiddle standing against the porch wall,
got in the truck without my asking.

Larry's Anecdotal Evidence 40

There was a girl that disappeared,
and the cops come out to the house,
thinking it might have been Sam
because he was dealing a lot and
to them that meant he could do anything.
It was a hot day, the dogs under the porch,
and Sam was pretty cool like a bad guy
in a Eastwood film, and there was something
in their voices; you could tell they was scared,
walking around the property,
kicking a tractor tire, punching hay bales
in the barn loft, looking for tracks that
might lead to the woods; and when they left,
I said, "Sam, what the hell have you done?"
But Sam just sat there and looked at me
like I might be one of them; then he lit up
a joint, watched the sun set across
the valley, and we both sat there
in the deafening silence.

Larry's Anecdotal Evidence 32

Those first weeks after her stroke,
before Medicaid kicked in,
I home-cared for my momma.
She laid in the bed, her mouth
hanging open while I sipped
bourbon and smoked crystal and
weed and watched satellite porn.
Her skin was soft and splotchy,
and I was tempted to burn her
to see if she reacted
and for all she let Daddy
do to my brother and me.
She had broke her glasses some
time, and her eyes always kept
that unfocused look you see
in winos and the deranged.
The whole house smelt of piss
and sweat and inhuman filth,
and I knew I had to get
her gone to the county home
the night I held my pistol
to her sleeping head and prayed
for the courage to fire it.

Larry 14

When my brother left the farm
for the Lord, I let the fields
go for the first year, cooking
instead; Uncle Burton's old
Oliver stayed in the lower
meadow where I ran it out
of gas. No lime, no hay cut,
the prickly pears sprouted down
the old fence line. The gas mask
left red lines on my fat face,
and I sold to the worst trash
I thought I'd ever see. When
I finally mowed, I got
two flat tires, but I paid the
last of the land off and bought
a new baler I could use
by myself, when my brother
gave up the farm for the Lord.

Larry's Minacious Dream

I swear, Artemus, it was like a dream,
and I recall my hopes was that,
'cause I saw all these preachers
slobbering over their Bible verses,
lips glistening chicken grease,
the floors of their holy buildings
opening up to swallow them
in a bloom of blackness
so dark I could not see into it,
and yet I heard their brutish screams,
their Why Me Lords as they sank
into the pit; then I blinked—
I remember thinking, if I blink
maybe I can shed myself of this horror—
but then I saw all the queer rights folks
in their elbow-patch jackets
and sweater vests, their chests
thrown out like roosters of protest;
and, Artemus, I hoped it was a dream,
I hoped it out loud as the street
parted its asphalt lips and they sank
into the black bubbling sewer,
their faces gone white like in a movie,
and they screamed but they had no voice
like my brother Sam when the Old Man
raised his belt to welt his legs,
and then I awoke and sifted
through the drama to see where I stood
and what it might mean, Artemus,
as I know that dreams are what
floats to the top, that no divine
strings pull them, like metal pails
slapping the sides of the darkest wells.

Larry's Birthday

There's a sickness that rises in my gorge
that the money and the women can't quell,
and I heave on my knees as the sunrise
oranges over Burton's granite bluff,
and the sadness of the abandoned fields
is my only blanket against the chill,
that and the first seizure of smoke
that fills, then levels,
though I feel like the whole
empty house of this world
waiting on a god
to blow in
the next storm.

Larry's Anecdotal Evidence 88

I flashed my gold-tooth smile
at the guy in the guard house
and idled the pickup out past
the tennis courts, the swimming pool
covered for the frozen winter,
building after building of college apartments
adorning the bulldozed ridge.
I parked Visitor at BB-4 and crunched
my work boots on the ice-topped snow.
Goddamn, it's cold, I thought,
focusing my eyes on the door number
before I knocked. The construction
was impossibly cheap, and even
in the constant wind I could hear
music from within, the thump
thump thump of a hip-hop beat,
and I knew they were there,
with or without my money.
I checked my pistol in my right
waistband, felt the hawk bill
in my left pocket, mumbled
my good luck saying,—"Lord, forgive
me for what I am about to do,"—
and then it was my red knuckles
against the blue metal door,
echoing all the way to Hound's Ear.

Larry's Anecdotal Evidence 89

I stood on that busted millhouse porch
watching the full moon inch through a walnut tree,
listening to the river refinding rocks
over and over below the concrete dam.
Finally, I pushed the door open slowly,
knowing he might be sitting the dark
in his overalls, a shotgun across his lap;
but there was naught, and I walked
the front room through,
kicking an overturned cat bowl,
my boot crunching something gravelly.
In the back room I saw two pairs of eyes,
a diapered walking baby and a young girl
in a burlap dress with matted blonde hair,
both of them pale, weasel-faced.
"Where's your pappy?" I said, but she just
looked at me like she didn't know words
while I searched for something that might
be worth taking and found nothing.
Back on the porch, I saw her haunted face
watching me through the one window,
and the moon had climbed to the top
of the walnut tree where it nested
like a whole 'nother world of spun gold.

Rough Beast

The singer's T-shirt covered
a bright red Tasmanian
Devil tattoo, leaving the
feet hanging out like it was
trying to land on his elbow.
"Tattoos are rebellious," I said,
winking at him and punching
his shoulder a bit too hard
like a first baseman on a
pickoff attempt; right away
he wanted to be rid of me,
so I sat down at his table.
"I'll have whatever he's drinkin',"
I told the waitress, and I saw
him tilt his head, searching the room
for a bouncer; I think I just have
a way with people though 'cause
he took my card and said yes
to everything I asked, and when
I left, he looked pretty happy
about our deal or my leaving
and I locked his eyes when I
shook his dishrag of a hand
so that what I meant sank in.

Laureate

Laureate Larry

The *Farm Poems* became a
bestseller and the *Atlantic*
Monthly called Larry a hardscrabble
genius and the next point in America's
poetry constellation while the
New Yorker called him a dirt farm
Bukowski and *Harper's* deemed him
the most honest man in America.
Larry cashed the checks
and got his teeth fixed and
bought the biggest, most obnoxious
truck he could find,
refusing to fly
on his first book tour.

Luminary

When Larry went to his first literary conference,
he sat behind the end of a table in a semicircle
of writers, all eager to sign their books for the
attendees who grazed the book tables in the
adjoining room. But Larry didn't try to be nice
or to charm the strays that wandered over
to him. An elderly woman in a wheelchair
pushed his book across the particleboard
surface and gushed, "I just love the utter
bluntness of your poetry, Mr. Ledbetter."
Larry signed it, *Fuck you, rich old bitch,*
Love, Larry, and handed it back to her,
saying "I think they should put you to sleep."
The events director at the small mountain town,
already having fielded numerous complaints,
approached Larry. "Do you have any suggestions
to improve our festival, Mr. Ledbetter?"
"Get rid of the writers," Larry replied.
The state's poet laureate, a couple tables
over, labored over his latest monologue,
not daring to look over at Larry's table,
a situation he was somewhat responsible
for as he had, while teaching poetry in
the prisons, met Larry and convinced him
to "put his life in words." "You got any Vicodin?"
Larry asked an odd little woman who wore
a purple wool hat that tied under her chin.
Another reading or workshop or lecture
was scheduled for the room, the other
writers having left as soon as the time
was up, most having sold no books, but

Larry refused to leave. "Y'all just go ahead
and do what you want," he told the
volunteers who rushed to reset the room.
"I like this part. I'll just sit here and sign
books till I'm through," and so he sat, his back
to the poet laureate who was about to read
in a room that the audience feared to go into.

Luminary 2

"So you the last American man,"
Larry said, stepping forward
to the table where the famous
mountain man sat, explaining
to festivalgoers how momentarily
he would ignite yet another fire
with nothing but sticks.
"I used to poach turkeys on your land,"
Larry said, holding his hat in hand
like a neighbor who had come to call.
"Just thought I'd let you know because
I've kind of got a hankerin' for some turkey,
and since I'm up here signing my
poetry books anyway, I thought I might
make a side trip." The mountain man's face
turned red, and he looked like he might
come across the table, but something
in Larry's eyes stopped him and Larry
sensed a hollowness he had always felt
encountering con men in prisons and
churches. "Well, I'll be over here, Mr.
Last American Man," and he smiled
a sad smile, resetting his hat and
ambling back to his own table.

Larry's Pragma

"I used to watch Uncle Burton whittle,"
he told one interviewer right out there
on the porch, "and he would just be gloomy
when he started, then he would get focused,
and you knew he could see, not the wood block,
but the object stuck inside, and begin
to cut it out. Well, it's the same for me
with these poems—I lay it all out, the words,
I mean, and then carve to find the damn poem."
As he talked, Larry had drawn his belt knife
and held it before the interviewer's
face like he was making a point with it.
Then he lowered it to halve a white pill.
"Here, you can have some, if you like. You see,
it ain't Whitman for me. It's Vicodin."

Larry's Hypothetical

He'd been told that a writer has to have
a theory or his work is meat without
a skeleton, so he thought and he thought
because he knew it was most important
till finally he imagined it all up,
and he explained it later, during what
are often referred to as his genius
years, what he called the crime poetry theory.
"You see, most writers give readers something,
but my work takes things away instead," he
said, "and if you keep reading, before long,
without me, you've got nothing left, and then
nobody else's work is good enough
to make you feel the kind of bad you need,
and it may seem like a crime because that's
what it is—in fact all poetry is."

Larry Discusses the Biz

I must say something about my publisher.
He's a tool, a journeyman nobody
who didn't know what he had
when I sent him the first book;
and I have threatened him more
than anybody besides my brother,
but he doesn't have the sense
to be afraid. He's like the plainest
hog in the lot who suddenly
gets all the slop, and he doesn't
care how it happened; he's just
the hog with all the slop.

Larry's Anecdotal Evidence 78

You know I'm not crazy about poetry readings,
but they pay the bills, and sometimes I'm asked,
by other writers "what's the craziest reading
you've ever done?" Those are the kind of things
writers talk to each other about, sort of like
professors complaining about students, but when they
ask you something, it's always because they've
got some mad story that they think will top yours;
that's how they are, but anyways, I was one time
asked to do a reading for a reunion of former
bank employees who shared the experience
of being my hostages during a failed robbery
some twenty years before, and I felt compelled
to behave myself, so I read and talked real nice
like Andy Griffith, and I told them that I hoped
that the next time that I had to take hostages
that they would not be a part of it. As I phrased
out the meanness of my poems, I watched
their eyes, and I could see how much they loved me;
and I knew that the act for which I had paid my years
had made them more—more than they could have been.

Larry's Anecdotal Evidence 6

I was reading for one of them MFA things,
you know, where they raise up poets
in small herds like a bunch of ball-less hogs.
This one was somewhere in Mississippi,
and there were some beautiful scared-looking
youngin's in the group, and when I got
to the question-and-answer part, I began
to size them up the way I might a bunch
of hogs; and I knew I had set a spark
in a few of them, but they had to wait
for their professor to ask the first question,
which she began after the traditional pause,
"Mr. Ledbetter, what do you recommend
for a person to do to become a success
in the poetry world?" I had watched this
one already, a skirt a bit too short,
flirty in the ways you can feel in the air
around her as if in competition with
the young coeds in the group. "How long
you been married," I asked. "About twelve
years," she said. "Would you leave your
husband for two weeks of your life with me?
That's what it would take," I said. I wish
I'd had a rattlesnake to throw on the floor
at that point, you know, just to break
the tension in the room. I'd a liked to see
all them long skinny white legs
scrambling to the tops of their desks;
but I didn't have one, so I just smiled
my best university MFA program smile
and asked for the next question.

Larry Anecdotal Evidence 57

I married a poetess,
and we moved back to the farm
where we sit the porch some nights
and make plans for an orchard,
one like Burton used to have,
and I tell her how much I
like a cherry cobbler and
fried apple pies, and I will
use some speaking money to
buy the kind of trees Burton
could never afford; and when
he looks down from the cowlick
of stars, he'll see the straight
line of staked saplings and
he'll hear my hippie girl
laughing and meditating,
and he will know I figured
it out or got damn lucky.

Larry's Review of the *Penguin Poetry Anthology*

I've got nothing against this big bag of shit.
Men have always slicked each other to no end.
Think of cheap cigars, stale office air, dollops
of despair, endless crying jags, circle jerks,
men who never pulled a briar from their britches.
It's like the difference between fantasy
football and real football, but don't take my word;
support the arts and further the scam because
I've got nothing against this big bag of shit.

Larry's Anecdotal Evidence 84

He had that look like somebody
who'd never been hit by a fist in his life,
a thin stubble of beard on a baby face,
and I knew his hands were soft
without shaking, so I stood back
in a corner where I could watch
across a bookshelf of regional authors;
and he was like all the college boys,
talking about how he'd studied
his subject for weeks on youtube
and in some historically significant book
from the '60s, and in his case,
the subject was serpent handling;
and I smiled to myself because
I could tell he'd never held no rattler,
and I longed to sling one
across the room,
but I just slipped out the door
back to Haywood Avenue
before this New Voice of the South
could tell us just who he'd studied under.

Larry's Pragma 36

I have read about men and what
they have thrown away for art—
wives, families, church, friends—
and how devastating it was to let go
of what's safe and what's familiar.
I never had people or places
that thought of me as special;
a man was always a man found wanting
in some way sooner or later,
and I would be forced to measure
against what I needed or wanted.
Yet I have seen them shake their heads,
wondering what I must have lived
and how dispossessed I appear.
I am only an artist as much
as they believe it,
and I have given up nothing
I can't return to in darkness.

Larry's Requiem for Uncle Burton

Larry's Requiem for Uncle Burton

We can't talk about rare birds and rough stones
without summoning Uncle Burton's soul;
you see, he burned like the crackling pine that
sweetens the stale death in an old plank house,
and he heard the whispers of the long dead
walking the clover path in the meadow,
and he knew where he would go way before
the overturned tractor pinned him there
by the granite bluff where he prayed at night;
and now he's in those stars, Uncle Burton,
up above us over this valley, and
I can feel him shining his light on me
even now as I work my meanness like
spit in the face of this sorry world.

Larry's Divining

I've got on my muddy boots,
descending into the gorge,
thinking about a man I
should kill but probably won't.
I stumble through storm shrapnel,
broken limbs, an old metal
cable grown into the trunk
of a battered hickory.
Soon I smell the laurel and
hear the creek gurgle beyond
the green thicket of briars,
see the rock-slick single track.
I will stand in the clearing
across the swimming hole where
Burton planned his pout house
till an answer settles me.

Larry's Poems of Place 3

There is no ground to give some nights.
A death is like a lie retold
till the truth vanishes in it.
I do not want to want the past,
for death lives there in a shadow,
but I walk to the moonlit bluff
and stand there in Burton's long coat,
wanting every bit of it back.
There is no ground to give some nights.

No Motion Without a Void

I swear the fields never looked no better
than when you mowed in middle November,
racing the Massey hard to get it done
before gloaming yellowed over the pines,
the bush hog spitting briars and stubble,
not thinking about nothing else but the
tightening brown oval of trimmed whiskers,
then standing under stars by the fire pit
with a whisky, admiring the clean view,
not thinking about a damn thing, again.

Larry Gets in Touch with his Feminine Side

Just because I'm not afraid of my words,
or rather their effect, doesn't mean that
nothing moves me; there's a way the dusk light
breaks through the pines at Uncle Burton's bluff
that makes me feel like my boots are floating
above the chalky dirt and milky quartz.
I have watched a deer stare across the same
distance, so still, never an animal
I needed to shoot to prove my man-ness.
I have set around campfires in freezing
winter and heard scared men tell the pure truth,
brothered as wolves might be if not for the
dark engine of hunger and the rattle
of death; and I know any snake can swim
beautiful eses in a cold river,
but a lying man leaves a careless trail
like mice scrambling in a freshly cut field
where a boy with a loaded pistol
and some time is a comfortable god.

Larry's Line

I know my number is coming;
a man can only risk so much,
and I can hear the drums of their
footsteps thudding, boots kicking
leaves and gravel and black mulch,
and I can only hope they face me
so I can see their guns sparking
for that microsecond before,
not surprised from behind at a
campfire by a cowardly sniper
and my blood splattered among
red maple leaves mixing with
black dirt and moss and pine resin.
My number is coming, and it
is speeding toward me like the earth
and the stars and all the crazy seasons.

Larry's Anecdotal Evidence 84

I was mowering
in low gear
back down pasture
where the dry breeze
whiskered through
brown tarantula grass
when there was a sky flash
like a struck piece of metal,
and my light went out like the time
Sam conked me with the calf bucket.
When I roused,
my face was mashed into the mica dirt,
the Massey parked and idling,
its hog lift raised.
I sat myself and
studied the afternoon:
bright sun, blue heavens,
squirrels scampering
in the oak woods.
Well, I thought about
some son of a bitch
hit me with buckshot
and I thought about god
smited me like Sam always said;
then I thought as I got back on
this is just the kind of stuff
that happens to me—
and it was.

Going Away Is Harder Than I Thought

I thought I could just go down to the woods
and be done with it, or that playing dead
would just become second nature,
like driving to work or rolling
the garbage can to the road.
I know; you always bury a copperhead
because you don't want to be stung
by the yellow jackets that eat it.
But who can bury all the poison
a man turns loose in this world,
and is it better to leave a few people at a time
or to go in one big humanitarian blast?
Morning, I look in the mirror
at the ruin that's left, measuring
the evil that casts its own reflection:
who's gonna die today, Fat Boy,
me or you.

Larry's Anecdotal Evidence 85

King of Darkness

Nights I'd sit the barn loft
amongst the hay bales
to watch the moonlight
drift between the eave slats,
outlining my bearded face and
shoulders on the back wall,
and I'd wonder about God
and the terrible secrets
men carry to their graves,
and the joint's orange glow
was just the tiniest bit
of hell poking through.

Larry's Pragma 33

Since nobody knows what Jesus looked like,
you can make up whatever you want:
blue-eyed, dreamy, speaker of perfect English.
I've been here and there and studied on it
a bit, heard my brother's pronunciations,
and I have closed my eyes and mumbled
drunken prayers, and I have felt something
cold pass through me when a man expired,
and I have felt something lift from my shoulders
when there was nothing there to see,
and I have looked long at my hairy reflection
in rivers and mirrors and thought that maybe,
just maybe, Jesus looked a lot like me.

Larry's Pragma 56

I've seen men behold their whole lives
to promises made to the dead,
thinking that approval could be won
beyond the grave or that a man's
death should be happy and tidy
like the end of an old movie.
But it was never meant to be
anything but messy, my daddy's
brains blown against
the hard gray barn-loft planks
so that when I stacked the hay bales
I would always think of how
I found him pitched backwards,
his dentures and one of his eyes
laying where the blood had pooled
and dripped through the floor
into the hog feed; and I never
promised him nothing, never would
have, and I am beholden to no
pathetic man, no jealous woman,
no greedy rule-writing god.

Laureate Larry's Pragma

We're just some people
living on a planet somewhere;
anything beyond that is guesswork.
I'll hold the ladder for you
if you'll hold the ladder for me;
maybe we can get a better look.
When I climb into the barn loft
before I move the hay bale,
I know the snake is there.
When I watch the night sky
above the field out beyond
the fire pit, I become convinced
that, good or bad,
great or small,
alone or in fiery processions,
we fall
up there.

Larry's Secondary Musing

We live in layers,
the mountain's mossed rocks,
four wheeler moonscape grooves,
horse tracks sunk in the watershed's
leaf-covered slime.
Some nights the years
unbury themselves in my head:
Burton in his unbuttoned shirt
standing atop the hay wagon;
Sam barefoot in overalls
running from the Angus bull;
Papaw teaching me to sight a gun
out by the rabbit briars;
girl cousins in the hayloft
slicking us with naked dares;
and under it all the Catawbas
hunting silently before the fields.
How I try to keep it there
with the layers of what I've done,
sometimes right as Christ,
more often bob-wire bad.

Larry's Poems of Place

This porch is where I spit;
that yard is where I piss
under a moon like tonight's,
watching the neighbor's
white reindeer lights.
Even from here
by the grapevines
where I stand uneasily,
I sense the contours of darkness
hovering over the terraced field.
No evil moves me.
I spark a joint
or I don't.
The black slow dance.
Maybe this is
some kind of love.